LEARN THE VALUE OF

Manners

by ELAINE P. GOLEY

Illustrated by Karen Park

ROURKE ENTERPRISES, INC.
VERO BEACH, FL 32964

Library of Congress Cataloging-in-Publication Data

Goley, Elaine P., 1949–
   Learn the value of manners.

   Summary: Provides examples of good manners and demonstrates through two brief stories how they can be used at home and when playing with friends.
   1. Etiquette for children and youth.
[1. Etiquette]   I. Title.
BJ1857.C5G65   1989   395'.122   88-4532
ISBN 0-86592-395-7

Manners

Do you know what **manners** are?

It's **good manners** to say "PLEASE" when
you want something.

Saying "THANK YOU" when someone does something for you is **good manners.**

When someone says, "THANK YOU" to you it's **good manners** to say "YOU'RE WELCOME".

It's **good manners** to introduce your friends to each other.

When you say: "Mom, that was a great meal,"
that's **good manners.**

It's **good manners** to put something back when you're finished with it.

When you meet someone for the first time, it's
good manners to say: "I'm very glad to meet you."

Holding your knife and fork correctly
is **good manners.**

It's **good manners** to cover your mouth when you cough or sneeze.

Good manners means not talking with your mouth full.

It's **good manners** to say: "Hello, Smith residence,"
when you answer the telephone.

Good manners means really listening when someone speaks to you.

21

Saying "HELLO" when you see someone you know
is **good manners.**

It's **good manners** to let someone walk through the door before you do.

Putting your dirty clothes in the clothes basket
is **good manners.**

Not interrupting when someone is speaking
is **good manners.**

It's **good manners** to take turns when you play
a game with someone.

Good manners means being polite!

Manners

Fred and Joan had just finished their supper.

"I want some cake!" shouted Joan.

"Please, Mom, can I have a piece of cake?" asked Fred politely.

"Okay, okay," said their Mom. "Help me clear the table and I'll cut each of you a piece of cake."

"I want a bigger piece!" shouted Joan.

"Thanks, Mom." said Fred.

How did Fred use **good manners?**

How did Joan show her bad **manners?**

How can you use **good manners** at home?

Manners

Tim and Gary were playing checkers. Each boy took his turn.

Then Alan came over and said, "I want to play. Move over, Tom, so I can play."

Alan took one turn, then another.

Gary said, "Alan, it's not polite to push someone out of the game. I don't want to play anymore."

Alan shouted, "I want to play! Stay and play with me!"

Tom and Gary left the room.

How did Alan display bad **manners?**
How can you use **good manners** when you're playing games with your friends?